CW01337414

blessed

Modern Haibun on Almost Every Despair

Andrew Riutta

blessed

Modern Haibun on Almost Every Despair

Text © 2022 Andrew Riutta
Cover Image © 2022 Mark Meyer

ISBN 978-1-958408-07-0

Red Moon Press
PO Box 2461
Winchester VA
22604-1661 USA
www.redmoonpress.com

Special thanks to Janet Lynn Davis
and Rich Youmans for copy editing,
and to all the editors who
have found value in my work.

First Printing

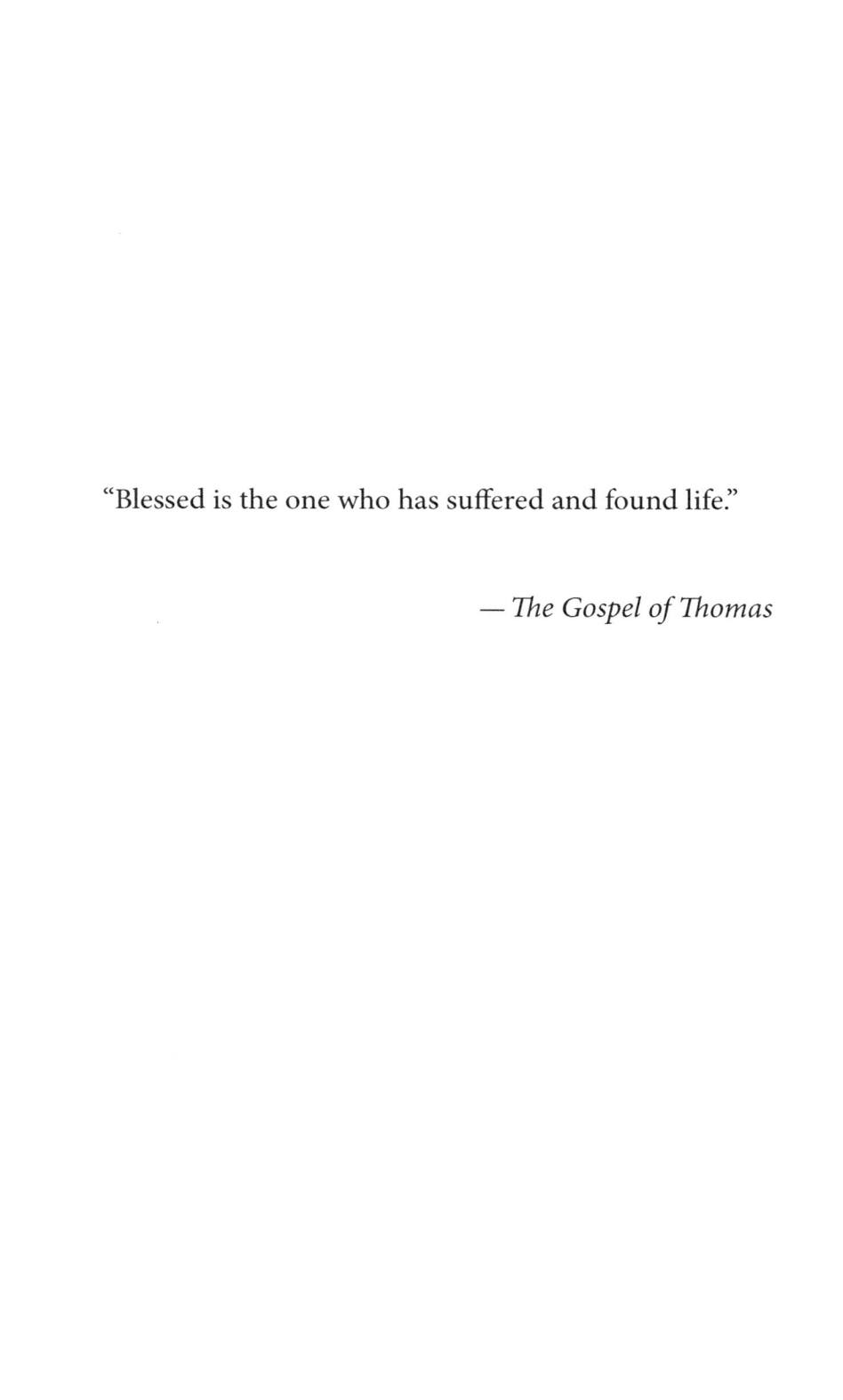

"Blessed is the one who has suffered and found life."

— *The Gospel of Thomas*

blessed

Old Crow Charlie

One night, he woke me by hacking so hard in his bedroom below that I almost called 911. It went on and on. At one point, I thought I even heard him crying. But it all finally let up after about an hour. So I went back to sleep.

I got up the next morning and made coffee. He came hobbling into the kitchen with a bottle — and a grin like he'd just robbed a clam of all its pearls.

"Ain't no way that Meryl Haggard ain't a damn god," he said.

His eyes were so red he looked part demon. He dug through the fridge for some cold venison, mumbling that he missed his wife more than his mother.

He headed back toward his room, then turned in the doorway before entering, toasting the heavy air.

"But not more than this."

>   in a nightmare
>   Bibles stacked so high
>   they fall and crush me

[for Charles Foust]

Life Out of Balance

I light a cigarette in the dark inside my camper while the wind blows fiercely through the hills and its stars. "Koyaanisqatsi," I say to myself. It's nearly four in the morning but I can't stop thinking about that old Native woman with no indoor plumbing who had an eagle feather dangling from a crucifix on her kitchen wall. She said that, when the Lord comes back, she will give him that feather and a bowl of corn soup and maybe then Mother Earth's tumors will go back to being butterflies and she and her people can be people again. I don't remember if she said anything else.

>   instant coffee —
>   I swallow the crack
>   of dawn

[*for Hazel McSawby*]

Dear John

How have you been? Did the days and seasons follow you there? Do clouds come casual and soft, like lilacs, or does it seem they want to murder you some more? Are there any profound valleys nearby, like you went to in Wyoming — rivers or streams perfect for your casting and delivery? Do you still have that sharp pain in your arm from when you fell off the roof?

How about the floaters in your eyes? Were they, in truth, just the ghosts you couldn't avoid, especially your mother? Can you get a sense of the whole story now?

Do you miss your sailboat, its incalculable worth caught in golden sunlight? Do you miss your deepest pulse?

And does the scent of that young bartender's perfume yet float for you? Still make you want to roll around in the dirt like a dog?

>Hunter's Moon —
>the bone-chilling sound
>of an empty tin cup

A Copper Country Romance

My first girlfriend's name was Wanda. She was born with a missing index finger, though she still had one to point and blame. Which she did. But it was never my fault. Blame the morning, for it is here. Blame anyone and anything.

Blame the four winds. Blame Ma and Pa. New love screams in the faces of those who devote themselves wholly to its mammalian scents. I glanced up at a robin when I should've been worshipping her thirteen-year-old curves.

I was caught skipping stars across the darkness when she wanted me to focus on her music. This is the dance that twirls itself to the lunatic noises of lust and let down.

This is the beautiful sky at dusk — purple as a shiny bruise.

>
> Fourth of July sparklers —
> a shadow
> of us

Sober

For six months now, I've been wringing out my brain. And liver. Simple as that. The moments at hand are the moments at hand. Nothing more. And I suppose that ought to be good enough — perhaps as good as it will get, anyway. Used to be I'd get drunk, and everything was so alive and multidimensional. Interchangeable. I could dance the same dance listening to Willie, Ravel, or Lady Gaga.

I'd float in all the cracks with a warm smile and, thank God, booze raised to the stars. Now the days are kind of like eating hardtack. Eating hardtack with bad teeth.

But still, there's something to be said for the unclouded virtues that things possess. Today, a strawberry smells like a strawberry and not a woman's saliva. Speaking of love, well, don't ask. If I had a bottle, the crow in the maple tree outside my window would likely have all the answers.

But I don't. So it doesn't.

> hunting for beach stones,
> I hit the jackpot . . .
> three plain rocks

[*for Ed Markowski*]

Victory Song

My dear friend and former college professor is dying at home in his bed while the trees are turning red, yellow, orange. First it was academia and a much-younger wife.

Then yardwork and sailing. Now shivers inside a thin sleeping bag that will perhaps be recycled into his coffin's lining. I think I could get used to the darkness more than not being able to breathe. Or suppose after death God gives us each a heavenly snorkel or cuts slits in our individual spirits so we can inhale the divine. Hallelujah. All I know is that we used to get drunk together and watch the skirts of lush female tennis players get shoved around by the wind.

Or sometimes we'd talk politics — but very rarely. I buried my old dog in his backyard and he painted her a nice stone, name and all. That's our story, and I'm pretty sure it's good enough.

> Indian summer —
> fish bones basking
> in a child's footprint

[for John Pahl]

The Makings of Kid Rock

Was going to listen earlier today to a live podcast of various poets responding to the coronavirus pandemic. Instead, I watched an old wrestling match on YouTube between Andre the Giant and Hulk Hogan — because the 80s was such a rockin' wild time in America, that's why. Ratt, Mötley Crüe and Cinderella. Lita Ford in tattooed pants and torn-up skin.

The Beastie Boys smoking everything. Madonna humping the whole wide world. Kenny Rogers rolling the dice on it all.

Warrant and their "sweet cherry pie" filling in the dry wall's cracks.

The scent of grass stains and corn dogs. Poetry came after all these things.

>   dusk —
>   the Tilta-a-Whirl flings
>   her warm smile

Lost and Found

If you ever find yourself on your way to a Native American sweat lodge because the spirit in you has for months been dwindling into a blatant existential sorrow — or maybe because you keep waking up with mild pain, some in your stomach and some in your chest — and your doctor doesn't have any answers, here are a few things to keep in mind as you drive to the rez:

1. The moon doesn't know you by the name on your birth certificate.

2. While you quietly undress you must empty your thoughts until your life is not even a whisper in the face of time.

3. The lodge itself is a womb and so you must learn how to give birth to yourself and then everything else.

4. Forget all politics.

5. Jesus was a medicine man.

6. Indifference can be a manner of caring on multiple levels.

7. The river beyond runs into the stars.

8. Don't pray, sing.

9. Thank your hosts afterwards by not wiping your face while you eat.

10. At this point, you are barely a ghost.

> cedar smoke —
> the woman with no teeth
> smiles at nothing

Civil War

Cold wind.

No more moonlight,

no more answers.

The neighbor's dog with a bone

that was the other neighbor's dog.

        crows . . .
        hard to tell if they are
        laughing or not

An Ex-Lover's Birthday

Mid-April, and, tonight, a rare event of thundersnow dominates our skies. Except for this, it's pretty much been an ordinary day, a Sunday of pancakes and sausages and flashes of birds going from trees to power lines. And then back. A few unassuming thoughts on the meaning of it all. But somewhere in those thoughts there's one that has kept trying to push its way to the front of the crowd, and now it seems it's finally broken through.

A memory — lying on that grassy hill, where I told her I would die without her. And here I am, almost forty years later, just living my life.

> toxic masculinity . . .
> he rips apart the earth
> to bury a mouse

William Muckinen

He said, "I sometimes wonder if the wind can feel itself, or what it's raging up against as it cuts through the meadow. Its strong gusts colliding with flowers. At least Helen Keller could poke herself in the ribs. Or touch a dead bird. She had that going for her. What if we had to take on all the pain and grief we gave others over the years — whether you meant it or not — in a single day? Could you survive? Heck, I know I couldn't. I'm a trooper of the Gospels but, no matter, I've had to breathe in my own burps quite a few times. It's God's way of saying, 'You're barely even a dying spark of the great fire that I am.' Or something like that. But then after a while he'll pat my back and tell me not to worry all that much about things."

>   blue sky —
>   fresh snow on the graves
>   of those I love

Lupus

My young niece sure wishes she could be rebuilt slightly bulkier. A bit more sturdy. Told me that she'd love to weigh another fifty or so pounds and feel what it's like to push through the day with booming hips. With some thunder and a bit of confidence.

After dialysis, she looks like a flower that's been pressed too long inside the pages of a book. Or a deer gaunt from winter, afraid of the wind.

> Worm Moon...
> her brave Pomeranian
> battling shadows

[for Jessica Chambers]

Chicago

I once wrote a poem about how some of its streets are so dark that even the marrow oozing from their hacked bones tries to turn around and creep back inside.

But my little girl drove there all by herself yesterday in a rusty, fifteen-hundred-dollar car because she wants to explore her options in this world. In this sheer existence.

Maybe even catch a bus to other burning stars. I sure hope she goes to see Van Gogh in the museum while she's there. And, as much as I want her to peruse the bright colors of his fantastical love, I hope his old crows and peasants remind her of home and that she suddenly realizes that the grand cultural parade she's been craving has been right in front of her all along. And we can talk about this epiphany while we swing and smoke together in the smoldering pink sunlight.

>   Google searching
>   another word for "hope" —
>   winter rain

[for Issabella Perdurabo]

Shush

A friend once said that words wear down life's magic with their insistence upon trying to capture and contain a moment. Yes, he said it out loud, but then after that, practically nothing for months. One time, we walked several miles at night in the woods behind his cabin without an exclamation, or even a mumble, from his lips. No uncomfortable whistling either. But every once in a while he'd stop and listen. Mostly frogs and crickets.

Then he'd look up towards the moon, stars, and God and "grin like a motherfucker," a phrase he liked to say quite often when he still talked. Maybe all his silence really had to do with the fact that his wife was cheating on him with some rich doctor with nice teeth while his own teeth were coming undone. Could be. The following summer, when they found him dead on the bathroom floor, his four-year-old son was trying to feed him a peanut butter sandwich, his mouth a sealed tomb of his final thoughts on the whole mess.

>cool evening mist —
>the neighbor's dog
>barks at nothing

>[for John Robinson]

Chinese Zen Poem

The wind is forceful this morning, so much that I fear it will push me all the way through and out of any remaining enlightened dreams I may still remember.

The grass itself is crushed — all earthly mud, frozen.

There are crows here set aside for Hell; they stare me down and make me try to envy them for their meat scraps.

I am a skeleton trapped inside a man, who himself is turning to meat.

Neither sun nor moon care about any of these things.

>   Ghost Supper . . .
>   an old Native woman
>   thins her corn soup

Small Gospel for Recovering Drunks

Bumblebees were sent by God personally to teach folks how to live for flowers. Just flowers. No need for a new career, car, love, religion, or dream. Or a plane or bus ticket to Massachusetts, Montana, or Mongolia. Or Mars, for that matter. Flower to flower to flower.

That's how you must find your way.

>   winter wind —
>   the old dying furnace
>   our only hope

Surviving Antarctica

At AA, they told me to keep it simple. That's the secret.

The moon is just the moon, but it is God's moon. And if you want to keep the booze from screwing over your head and heart, then you have to know the order of things in the world.

Your place in it. Plus every prayer better be soaked with your blood to show you mean business. No one else's no more. It's okay.

Just gently reach out to them and tell them you're sorry.

You fucked up. It got away from you. The wind was so cold and deadly. Still is, but you've cooked yourself down now to the remembered warmth of everything and everyone good that's brushed against you, and that's enough to keep you from becoming just another frozen shadow.

> clouds or mountains,
> my old sleeping bag
> with its stains

Sublimity According to Joseph Campbell

Get to your god by heading way too fast down a muddy Oregon mountain in a '78 Dodge with real bad brakes. "Throw down the music and dance, man." We'd just finished filling it with firewood and were headed back to the farm. I kept on going like nothing really mattered anyway. Frank rolled me a cigarette. It had humps in it, so he called it a camel. I laughed.

We'd both almost crashed and burned but we just kept laughing, maybe even crapped ourselves. And when we hit the very bottom, Buddha was there waiting.

    frozen plums —
    an Alaskan fisherman
    rings the dinner bell

[for Frank Wyatt]

Spring Sunshine

Jesus. I guess I never really noticed it before, but each drip of melted snow falling off the eaves practically digs its own grave in the thawed dirt. Not much hope in that.

>multiverse theory . . .
>somewhere else
>maybe I still have her

Health Expo

She wants me to quit smoking. Says all it's doing is stealing days from us. And I suppose I don't disagree. I already gave up drinking about a year ago. The best moment of my life.

I got so many things back I had lost. God, the budding trees and my only child. The taste of food and a will once more to bend to tie my boot laces. And I also received gifts I guess I never really had before. Incredible stuff. A small but easy-to-get-to-know row of sunflowers. The delicate wisdom of a half-dozen chickadees darting in and out of the elm saplings.

A refined and brilliant woman who yet possesses cave-painting thoughts and tattoos made of mud. On this bright sunny day, though, she's only studying the clouds gathering inside my chest and praying it doesn't begin to rain. She always talks of how sad and alone she feels whenever it does.

> dead June bugs . . .
> she hands him
> the broom and pan

Fertile Ground

Thursday morning. Finally, a day off to catch up.

While listening to a song called "Everything is Free," I stare out the window at three men sweeping sand across a parking lot and think of the time I'd tried to teach my five-year-old daughter the difference between sand and dirt. "Nothing can grow in the sand," I said to her, letting it fall through my fingers." But I was telling a lie. It was in a sandbox that I'd lost my virginity to the girl across the street. I was fourteen. I rolled off of her and reached up for my shirt and jeans — which I'd flung into a pine tree — and in doing so, stretched myself as tall as my father.

> the pins and needles
> of a sleeping foot —
> bright summer breeze

Nearing the End of Summer

Curious, but there are a couple of gorgeous dwarf sunflowers growing alongside the ferns in front of the house, the same variety I planted at the back property's edge last year, right after I sobered up.

Both morning and early evening, I would whisper my hopes to them. And to myself. Sadly, those beauties failed. But these two shine, without any concern, care, or soft-spoken dreams.

Maybe God put them there to remind me that my own sharpened will can get me nowhere and I may only completely submit to his if I want true joy. If I say I'm a believer.

Or could it simply be that they arrived in bird shit? Yes, in all likelihood, that's probably it — the metaphor itself one of Mother Earth's lasting gospels that I must learn and then teach.

> clouds and stars —
> I make room in my mind
> for my skull

Buddha Hood

These moonless, middle-of-the-night summer hours are always the most frightening. The little bunny cutting through the weeds and forest debris sounds like a bulldozer gurgling the blood and bones of all you know that is soft and tender. Young daughters. Aging moms, dads. Eternal lovers.

Grandmothers and grandfathers. Sick uncles and aunts. Best, best friends. But what can a man do? Well, he can sip his instant coffee until his heart's a jackhammer and then peel away the tin roof — exposing himself utterly to the cold, dangerous dark as well as the neighbor's broken porchlight flickering on his poor bald head. That's what he can do.

> morning thunder —
> the weight of Odin's ravens
> on my wrist

[*for Ken Bergman*]

Frugal to the End

I would so much love to press my face against days to come like a brave little boy staring down a mountain lion at the zoo through bulletproof plexiglass, teeth and nose dripping adrenaline.

But death, thanks to an addiction that lasted years and years, is already deep on its way to get me. Plus the neighbor's dog just started barking so — damned lightning and its crashes — it's probably here now. I'm burnt toast and the ugly brown fields don't disagree. They keep telling me not to even bother with buckling my belt. Just roll another cigarette while I'm still able and be like that one old friend who lives in the foothills of western Oregon. Become my own rocking chair. My own window to stare out of.

> stars and stars —
> a dozen cattails
> black as creosote

[for Keith Strom]

Nearing Profound Heights

Just two and a half months away now from two years of recovery. Of staring at myself in tin cups of coffee. Of learning how to be grateful for four cold walls and a roof. A camp cot and hot plate. Even the mice nibbling at the wiring all night. And the stains on my pillow. One looks like the Lord, but after he'd been dragged and hung. Dirt and blood. I leave it to be reminded — that I may wholly own myself and then somehow try to build my new quiet little house using these same damn bones that used to beat holes in the walls.

> dead ladybugs . . .
> he tries making love
> to the deep silence

War Song

Starlings, starlings, starlings. And crows. Only the end of August, and here they are, already preparing for an even deeper end. As am I. Got my 30/30 rifle in the corner. My new ax next to that. A whole field of sage in a small clay pot ready to neutralize all the evil spirits — the world's wickedness trying to pickle itself in our blood.

I want to be clear here and tell you that John Wayne was really not as horrible as everyone thinks. Even my Native father says so. At night, he watches bad westerns to fall asleep so he can dream of good medicine. This is true reconciliation. This is the actual universe — its gravity and propulsions coming together in our very own shadows, followed by an impossible outcome that would undo your further attempts at reason. Because you don't know shit. Just like I don't know shit. And God will never have a face. Heh-yah, heh-yah, ho!

> thunder —
> a small dog shivers
> at its own ghost

Message to my Sister

Hey, how's it going? I'd love to talk. Maybe later this evening. Right now, I have some errands to run. A couple of items to get. Mostly weed and kerosene. Because, last night, Russia started bombing Ukraine. And they've begun talking World War 3. Which means that things could get awfully jammed up in the coming days and weeks. Months. And I wouldn't want to be caught not having something to curl up with that could keep me feeling cozy and warm through it all. Remember when we were small and you found our father passed out on the living room floor, your special blue fur coat — turned into a mangled heap — his blanket and pillow? I quickly became the Incredible Hulk, my pajamas ripped through by mountain ranges of boyhood muscle. But, in the end — I'm so, so sorry — I couldn't rescue it.

    Easter Sunday —
    burnt toast cutting
    the rose perfume

[for Lynnette Kempf]

Weighing the Day's Gospels

Quite chilly and clear this morning—just a couple of visible stars hanging on in the coming daybreak. Hard to believe it's already nearly halfway into September, the baby robins from late May, by now, either all grown up and harvesting worms or reduced to a little residual bacteria sitting somewhere within the forest debris.

These past few days, it's the crows I've been hearing more and more. And the cicadas. "Only in death will all this sadness part" is what they're saying. Or something like that. I can at least try to make some sense of their songs. And I ought to because maybe it's good advice they're offering.

My grandfather always had something to say, about all of it . . . but mostly fishing and hunting. Or how to sharpen an ax: "If you can't skin a muskrat, then what good is it?" But when the doc told him he had to choose between dialysis or Heaven, he simply grabbed his hat and coat and headed back home to Grandma.

> northern wind—
> I anchor myself
> to myself
>
> [*for Jack Chambers Sr.; haiku by Lucia Fontana*]

Blind, Empty, Odorless

I keep purchasing these damn reading glasses from the dollar store and they just keep breaking, falling off my face. But there hasn't really been a voice worth knowing deeply since Jim Harrison went anyway. Both the eternal stars and raw death have been gutted — and then removed from all the books. And the glorious strippers in their Tyrannosaurus-skin boots and furry angel wings? Told to instead just wear a face mask that covers everything, the whole story of the journey of their bodies. Or to at the very least blot with talcum powder any sheen that might reveal their yearning for Elvis and God, which means also any tears.

>spring haze —
>I close my eyes
>to picture her thoughts

Ax

I picked it up a few days ago at the hardware store. I tied leather fringe on it to give some purpose to the wind. Using the grit and gravel of the earth, I sharpened it beyond anything. Then I polished it clean in crisp moonlight. My plan is simple: find this woman — white plumage growing from her blood-caked chest — and start working my way into her darkness. Her softest light.

>pulsating sky . . .
>the Milky Way's glitter
>on fire

My Personal Church Pew

Really, it's only a wooden shoe/boot-changing bench put together by a good friend some years back. And yet, simply said — in its smooth varnish sheen — just when it seems hope and its light have gone astray, after the sun has slid behind the fading poplars and the neighborhood dogs have begun to pace at the speed of their own crazed blood, the soft glow and warmth of the day somehow still hang on. And so I sit and ask for courage with grace.

>   deadly storm —
>   into the great wide winds,
>   our neighbor's beer cans

[for Ray Cook]

Eugene

I'm finally going to give them a try, these generic cigarettes that were gifted to me last week by a Native American friend from Canada. An NHL-certified ice technician by trade, he'd moved here to northern Michigan after accepting a job offer to teach his traditional language to children. But he's already gone back. Because — even in small towns — politics always trumps traditions. Before he left, he handed me these smokes, as well as some frozen fish sticks and chicken fingers.

Behind thick glasses, his eyes beheld all things with an equal respect, making a fish stick no less sacred to him than a beaded medicine bag. In fact, tonight, I will microwave those fish sticks and offer a prayer while devouring them. Maybe even chant. After I'm finished, I'll step out into the light of the waxing moon and smoke. Coyotes will begin calling to one another across the cedar swamp and the air will smell of smoldering braids of sweetgrass. A hot ash will fall from my cigarette and be caught by the earth. But — before its glow has completely faded — a handful of ancient ghosts will lean in from out of the surrounding darkness to try to warm their hands.

> autumn arrives . . .
> I bend to greet
> a stone in the mud

Halloween Love

Somewhat cloudy tonight—yet enough moonlight pushing through that, walking to the camper earlier, I could see all the dreary ugliness. Graveyard rats chasing eyeballs among the grubs. Someone scraping a requiem on barbed wire using someone else's shin bone. Grime you wouldn't even wish upon an earthworm. Do you see where I'm going with all of this, baby? Because, last week, you asked me to tell you where I see myself in twenty years. Truthfully, I'll more than likely just be dangling from your neck: a bit of ashes inside the medicine pouch I stitched by hand for you last summer, falling into its bottomlessness while yet reaching for your mouth.

    frozen stars —
    Ghost Supper candles
    flickering

The Toothless Buddha

Gibran and Bashō served with pork loin and apple chutney was how he lured the younger gals to his place on Friday nights. (He was fifty and had marched with King in Alabama, so when I say "younger" I mean they were in their 30s.)

I only went because my girlfriend had been invited and I knew that if I didn't, he'd be all over her. During dinner, he read a little from *The Prophet*. "I am in the heart of God." I wept in my food. Then I asked him if he'd teach me how to write poetry; I'd bring him to Native sweat lodges in return.

But — years later — we were simply at a picnic table listening to Henryk Gorecki's Symphony No. 3: "Sorrowful Songs." We were both older, especially him, staring at a few starlings in the bare silver maples and the autumn hills with their shadows. Earth was only a tumbleweed.

    to insulate myself
    from the brutal cold,
    a woman I do not know

[for Patrick Scott]

Antique Feminism

My grandfather on my real dad's side — an Upper Peninsula copper miner and lumberjack — practically had sledgehammer heads for fists and could easily pound a man giving him lip into the ground. Into the graveyard. But, one night, after he'd come home drunk and quite unhinged, a noticeable look of the Beast in his eyes — Satan, Lucifer, Beelzebub, Fallen Angel, Prince of Darkness, Father of Lies, call it what you will — my grandma simply hit him in the head with an aluminum frying pan and told him that, next time, it would be cast iron.

    2 a.m. fog —
    I gently reach out
    to lightning bugs

Grief All Around

There are shards of bone in the wind this morning. There are bulldozer sounds coming from the mouths of soldiers. And that potato-brained politician on television — the amount he's been bought and paid for spray-painted in bright red on the giant billboard behind him — just keeps talking and talking.

A medicine man told me years ago that the dust he'd fetched off the moon while wandering in a dream wasn't magical but, instead, cursed with all the cold darkness that comes with eternity. That it gave him a heart attack and caused his wife to divorce him. "No shit?" was the only thing I could say.

These days, I'm going to a hot psychologist that lets me bounce on her knee while staring down her blouse. Almost always, I see the men she's been in bed with peeking out. But I don't mind. She knows the same heavy metal ballads I grew up on and has even let me watch her try to tango to them. Sometimes it's beautiful and sad at once. Sometimes the feathers from her scarf fall to the ground and are taken by the wind.

> autumn orchard —
> the skull on my belt buckle
> so soft in the sunset

Gray and Muted Landscape

Poet Jim Harrison said that it's a writer's duty to speak for those who cannot speak for themselves. And so today, I would like to go ahead and speak for my dear, dear friend who died last fall. He wants to know how it is that a man who ran marathons through the tough old trees and overlapping meadows for decades and decades could fall so hard to a yard full of pinecones. To moldy peaches beneath the windowsill. To the universe of dust wrapping around the clock.

    in the sycamore grove,
    beer bottle caps
    staring at the stars

Ain't That Something

My grandfather liked to say it whether he was speaking of the good graces of the Lord or some brand-new doohickey made for straightening even the most bent of carpenter's nails. And so when I think of how I became a broken drunk sitting in the dark, rubbing two dead fish together — trying to reproduce the gentle warmth I'd lost — and how I finally found the deep ugly bottom and pushed firmly off and away, back toward the daylight, the heavens, and landed straight to where I now sit, I can't help but to hear those words as the purest form of gospel.

> blood moon —
> from a dying friend's cup
> he sips

Sad Story

The older he becomes, the more deeply Scandinavian he looks, and that's just the plain truth. Sunken eyes not knowing what to do with the deadly sky that stretches way beyond practical measures and a limp that makes him dip with resignation towards the damp ground whether he's feeling cheerful or not.

When he was in is early twenties, he scrambled hard to have his appearance even slightly resemble the warrior characters from the movie *Dances with Wolves* — long pointed braids, pierced ears, and what he believed at the time to be a sharp countenance.

He wanted to frighten off the white man, the tourists with their speedboats coming from Cleveland and Detroit — and even local rednecks pounding beers and a gallon of vodka before trekking off into the trees to declare war on all the soft and fragile creatures.

But now happy little children themselves run from him, Old Man Who Rattles Ten-Thousand Skeleton Keys. And right around midnight — the poplar leaves whispering danger — he counts coup on stale animal crackers like his life depended on it.

>frozen fog —
>my old hot plate's glow
>a light in this world

Prayer

I told her gratitude is the key. Meaning, if you're craving a bright red popsicle but the freezer's offerings produce only orange, grab it while you can and say "thank you" from the deepest gully in your chest. Then say it again later — in the day, only this time with eyes closed to show God that you're not afraid of the dark because you understand how the divine light permeates all even when it can't be seen. (I once saw it in flashes in a strip club just outside Rapid City, Michigan, but I hardly ever mention that.) And before asking for another new toy truck for little Tommy or a cure for the crud eating away Aunt Betty's intestines, step outside and notice the pink sunset. And then the first handful of stars trickling in. Gratitude. Inhale so deeply, it makes you cough — cough up all the mess from the day's loves and losses, the throat made raw and tender. And then say thank you once more.

> using only the sparks
> from my empty lighter
> I cross midnight

Dark Winter

There are moments it feels that I must get a lot healthier — ought to quit smoking and eating just potato chips for supper — if I want to keep up with the Lord. Indeed, he leads me into green pastures, but other days he likes to bring me up and over piles of snow tall as a three-story farmhouse. Whenever he does, though, I always try to peer out over the years to come on Earth in hopes of seeing what may or may not be, in the end. But, today, it's so damned windy that I fear it could all get blown away well before noon.

> no stars tonight . . .
> alone in the closet,
> her pink kimono

1970 Something

When pushing down dead trees was good enough for our fun.
When old ladies solved most of the problems.
When phones were just for talking and the pink dusks held us captive
with dreams of raw and desperate love.
When nobody ever truly got hurt.
When a blue jumbo marble contained the universe.
When dirt roads mattered a heck of a bunch.
When country songs were made by those humbled by the Grace.
When a boy could be mistaken for a tumbleweed.
When the world could be fixed with a pair of pliers.
When owning one's own blood was the only requirement for everything.
When the color yellow led to affections more often than red.
When the wood thrush sang every important truth there ever was.
When a tired old bear could still roam the cold Lake Superior shores hunting for his own death.

> driftwood . . .
> such a long way
> to stillness

Recipes from the South

My real dad used to tell me to dream with a heart bigger than Mount Everest, but to always be okay with having leftover leftovers for supper. Actually, he never said that; or if he did, it was at the bar, and no one heard it over the jukebox and laughter. The clanking of bottles — raw and flailing souls of men and gals searching. Thus, my overall demeanor was mostly concocted in and out of the rat shit that covered the floors of our ugly blue trailer. I was more humble than a tumbleweed. I knew everything was stationed way up from me, especially the sun made of gold. But — God bless — there were folks over the years who could recognize this meekness for its beans and knew exactly how to make it shine. That old woman from Hazard, Kentucky, who taught me how to blend into the bright and colorful songs of dawn's cardinals, so gently, the sizzle of a country ham steak. "Just like that," she said.

> closing my eyes
> to gather its worth,
> a moonlit icicle

[*for Marcia Lynch*]

End of September

The time is now.
The time is now.

The Earth is ripe with vengeance.
Flowers curled up in themselves are holding daggers.
The wind has been given its course by the worms.
Inside a dead, hollow dog, the universe explodes. Expands.

"Aum," utters the Lord himself.

>   deep shade . . .
>   the medicine man
>   up to his chest in roots

Early June Rain

You can say what you want of the heart.

You can tell me that it is a nuclear bomb set to go off soon on bustling city streets.

You can tell me that it is a shiny piano in the hands of mother earth's darkest daughter.

You can tell me that it is a begging bowl filled with black husks.

You can scream that it has forgotten how to be a yellow butterfly (it's a sad old man shivering in a leaking rowboat).

And I would probably only agree.

> after a Ravel love song . . .
> the ocean inside
> a shotgun shell

Journal Entry of a Former Town Drunk

Saturday, May 15, 2021.

About an hour ago, tossing bird seed into the front yard — the maple buds giving a slight crimson haze to the moment — I pretended that I was God. That the seeds were stars and the ground I stood on, the universe itself. So, I tossed some here. A few thousand there. Then I looked towards the rising sun and said, "My oh my, you're really taking off, aren't you?"

It is the eye of all truth, at least any this side of four-and-a-half billion or so years. It was there when I was riding my bike with my friends deep in the woods and I fell behind and became lost. It said, "All your fears will soon build you so strong and sturdy, you'll spend hours of each day just talking to the cold. And it will teach you all about how to diminish my light."

>   flat dead grass . . .
>   a black face mask
>   among the starlings

Mother

Nearly thirty-six hours since I lit the Jesus candle I bought at the dollar store the other day and it's still burning, flickering like the stars sometimes do. Now that's money well spent. If, instead, I'd thrown it at a tall boy from the liquor store, things surely would have gone to the dogs and I don't mean like the three that are at your feet, so anxious for your peace and calm.

Just sit down already, Mom, and watch your television. Forget the dishes and laundry. We don't mind. Watch your soap operas and then your afternoon talk programs. Court dramas. Then your game shows. Then, finally, your evening news — your endless death counts of everything. Or get on Facebook and say hello to cousins and good friends. Marilynn, Kate, and Tom. Or look through your pictures of bright colorful birds and bursting sunsets. The best memories ever. Please, just relax . . . but while pushing up hard against us. Give us back our world.

        opening the blinds,
        she recalls her dream
        of a chaos of flowers

[for Linda Chambers]

Untitled

Middle of February and, outside, the snow just keeps piling up. My father, an old United States Marine, raises his handicap recliner so he can stand for the "National Anthem" playing at the Detroit Redwings game on television. He doesn't salute, but I can tell that he wants to. After Vietnam, they had him folding flags at funerals for boys whose jawbones had been blown right through their temporal lobes. Their very brains. These days, he eats microwave popcorn and listens to gospel songs on his phone. Willie, Billie Strings, classic Dolly Parton. He told me once that his legs have become so contorted and stiff from all the Agent Orange and arthritis, they'll probably have to snap his bones just to fit him into his coffin. "But Semper Fi," he said.

> Holy Bible . . .
> a cigarette inside
> flat as roadkill

[for Jack Chambers Jr.]

Oh Just a Book

After I'd texted her a picture of it — my mangled copy of Jim Harrison's *The Shape of the Journey* — she said, "What the hell is that?" And then I thought of all the things and folks and places the book and I had crawled in and out of together. Or simply collided with. The lilac groves and liquor stores. Moss-covered coyote skulls tucked in the backyard. Each day, after scraping itself across 10,000 miles of gravel and giving birth to the four cold and sacred winds, it just bleeds quietly on the oak shelf next to my Bible. For nearly twenty years, I have crucified it.

> just about midnight . . .
> my hangnail
> sharp as a thorn

Note to my Daughter

This morning I don't really know if I'm hearing a cicada out in the trees longing for another or just the sharpened silence of my own losses stretching to try to meet some kind of hope. Remember when you were maybe seven or eight and, one night, I helped you make an Albert Einstein hand puppet out of a paper lunch sack for a presentation in your class? After you went to bed, well . . . I drank about a dozen beers. And then begged him for all the answers. He gave me only a couple.

> Grandma's dog . . .
> just another old Buddha
> on crooked legs

Soldier in a Wheelchair

His mantra is the roar of a squadron of B-52s.

His hair is soaked to its roots with kerosene.

He lost one leg in the Battle of the Bulge.

He lost the other somewhere along the Ho Chi Min Trail.

Nearly every day, his wife tries to poison the 10,000 rats still chewing on his face. And he just stares out the window.

    winter wind —
    through a hole in the wall,
    an endless howling

The Makings of a Medicine Man

After I'd boiled it for years and years, the fluidity of love eventually became just a sticky mush.

Still, I went ahead and used it to try to seal the many cracks in my old house, only to realize it was in utter vain.

When the roof began to leak, I sat at the exact center of it all. Grew a few herbs where my hair used to be.

    crows —
    the dead suddenly
    more dead

Studying My Tobacco-Stained Fingers

They said I'd mostly have a grasp on it by now. They said I'd be bored with chasing bees to find the brightest flowers. They said I might even be old enough to know better about some things. And that God would tap my shoulder whenever my heart started wandering its deepest black thickets. Maybe that itself is our quietest faith. Our Holy Ghost. Could be but I'm not totally certain. The days struggle to translate themselves into apprehensible graces and glories. Except when she reads me Neruda. Spanish or Italian. She knows all the Romance languages. Even birdsong. Sparrow, robin, European starling. And right when the sun has begun to make its move and sneak up on certain poisonous clouds threatening from the horizon, she likes to call me long distance.

>	a stone arch
>	in front of the sea —
>	I enter the sky

Death Poem

November 3, 2020. Election day. Snow remains on the ground from overnight but the temperature is getting warmer. I light my kerosene heater anyway so I can get stoned off the fumes.

A thousand gunshots echo in the near distance...

I feel them in my chest. I feel my ghost in every movement—even stirring instant coffee. I step outside and stare at the moon in my cup... I give thought to softly making love to all her wounds. That's the kind of man I am. That's mostly what has been on my mind through all these years. Who will judge me?

> town drunk...
> a fallen branch
> his cane

He Who Knows Nothing Lasts

It's his Indian name, my sponsor in AA, and some recent unusual behaviors have had me concerned. Saying he can't make it tomorrow — truck is running poorly — only to call later in the day to ask if I want some trout he caught on Bear Lake. Skipping our coffee get-togethers because of the stomach flu, but then hours later sending me pictures of the gutted buck he shot hanging from the rafters in his garage. Its eyes black. Just black. I can't blame him. After all, two of his daughters were murdered in a single decade, and now his oldest doesn't speak with him. And so, if what I suspect turns out to be true . . . well, then . . . He's my old buddy, though as I type this, autocorrect keeps insisting that he is my old "buddha."

    black leafless trees —
    smoking a cigarette
    I inhale snowflakes

[for Steve Easter]

Hubble Spots Jesus

Last week, while browsing the globe on my phone, I came across this crisp NASA image — a fifty-thousand-light-year slice of our enormous galactic neighbor, Andromeda. When I zoomed in, it was nothing short of profound. I recognized that even the nuclear-fueled stars are themselves but pixelations caught inside the relentless unfolding of time; are no more determining or significant in the grand measurement of eternity than dust motes on a shoebox. I showed it to my old biker pal/ gospel brother, his ankle still gimped up from his most recent earthly collision. "Amen. All glory to God," he said joyously. "Now check out my new bong."

> Blue Öyster Cult
> on a hand-crank radio . . .
> white clouds in the birdbath

[for Douglas Kruse]

Chinese Zen Poem II

Not Elvis but mostly a quite pathetic Elvis impersonator.

Not one to climb Everest but instead a man scraping the bottom so he can more easily dream of — and then contemplate upon — the glories of standing at such heights.

Fifty years old and here I am living in a musty camper, feral beard inching towards the filth of the earth.

Just about every day, crows at the trash cans sing songs about me and laugh.

The falling snow is mostly silent, covering up so many screaming scars.

>   dark winter —
>   her Good News Bible
>   right beside her ashtray

[for Fay Kemppainen]

Cold

October 12 — just a couple more weeks till Halloween. One of the most chilling things I've ever witnessed was a hockey referee — his Covid mask also striped black and white — scraping with a metal chopper at two pools of blood that had seeped into the ice and then froze. I watched this while passing by on my Zamboni. I said to myself, "Is he qualified to do that? Does he have a special degree or something? Is he wearing surgical gloves? What on earth shall he do with it? Should it be treated sacred, like ashes? Or will he just toss it into the drain?" I went by him again and some small children on the other side of the glass just kept waving and waving at me, hoping for a warm, joyous honk.

    waning moon —
    my cigarette's glow
    my hallelujah

Irene

My grandmother must have brought it over with her from the old country, the recipe for making a home:

>   stacked Bibles and tarpaper
>   a can of lard
>   then three feet of snow piled on top
>   a corner for the sewing machine
>   a spot to hang Jesus
>   the creak of every door that opens and closes
>   the word for "hope" in Finnish
>   a stiff finger to break the soil
>   one apple tree
>   two daughters
>   a dead son
>   a faithful husband

Finally, a Formica table to roll it all out. To flatten the dimensions . . . to bring heaven closer to the earth.

>   endless road —
>   the sky curves
>   into blackbirds

[for Irene Riutta]

Romance in the Trenches

Love imagines itself divine and swirling when, really, what we mostly want to do is get filthy with one another in the brown weeds under the mind-boggling stars. "I'm your caveman, woman." Your hair's a trainwreck because I've been slamming you for years against the lavender dawns. You stand there dripping wet. I fry you an egg. I shovel it into your mouth, as any hard laborer would. The bills are everywhere but we're ashamed of nothing. Happiness surely couldn't ever get any grander.

>beech tree:
>a pocketknife exclamation point
>next to a heart

>[*for Lucia Fontana*]

Clearance Rack

I got this nice green weatherproof writing journal from the hardware store the other day while I was out shopping for a new ax. Figured I could jot down some notes on things like the weather, lunar phases, and such. And the lush garden I pray will come. Or even a few random thoughts about the Covid and how it relates to love and freedom. Death and us. Similar in tone, maybe, to what Santoka gave birth to on some of his travels. That kind of raw brilliance. But, to fulfill this, I may have to become a raging drunk again and pass out in the street trash. Yell rubbish about Buddha and his groupies. All because of a notebook that was 50% off.

>May snow . . .
>earthworms find warmth
>in the throats of robins

The Upper Peninsula of Michigan

> "We believe we have a life. We do not. It is Life in whom we have our being."
> — *Lewis Sawaquat*

You cast yourself out into a moment because that's really all there is to do.

Everywhere you look, there are dragonflies skimming the pond. And weeds taller than boys who pretend to be soldiers.

The sun had been up there a long time — maybe a thousand hours — along with all of its blackbirds and barn swallows.

But now a chilly haze brings with it into the early evening scents of mint and cedar. And smoke.

A yellow dog named after its antics bursts out of the shadows, wanting to chase or be chased.

You don't know it yet, but one day you will fall down in front of a woman and beg to be born into all of this once more.

> summer's end —
> I empty the bottle
> of all its purpose

Hallelujah 2019

That late spring, I somehow managed to find my recovery in an old, abandoned camper that was overrun with fading love stains and black mold. But also, loose plastic silverware, tea candles, window cleaner, masking tape, a homemade first aid kit in a Ziplock bag, empty grocery sacks inside empty grocery sacks, yellow yarn, a pipe wrench, two rusted cans of green beans, one coffee can of cigarette butts, frames without pictures, books without words, and a needlepoint magnetic heart, only, it was glued to the wood paneling. One night, using a giant silver flask — the same one my dear sister had originally got for me so I could nurse like a baby boy — I baptized myself clean as the wind.

       Sunday morning —
       countless purple violets
       inside a Holy Ghost fog

The Samurai

I'll confess, I don't really know all of what it actually means to be one, but I'm pretty sure it's more than just swords and grunts. There's the whole tea ceremony thing that comes geared with its quiet contemplations. Meditations and such. Eternity, one falling leaf at a time. Buddha and all the cosmos in his skull, like some of those cool tattoos I've seen in magazines. Stuff like that. But my good friend somehow balances his crazy approach to it, wearing cowboy boots and a hat — dashing through one battle after another on a drifting horse. Or inside his used sports car, blood on all the angels' faces. Love, his greatest enemy.

>   lightning and stars —
>   fools we have been
>   in this brief glow

[*for Jason Gates*]

Radiation and Love

Being held hostage smack in the middle of one's own malignant debris is indeed to be swallowed by the earth. You learn to just let the crows dig you out of bed by your guts. You are old, rotting canned meat. Not much else now. And your mind is cooked squash. But then you hear Ray Charles on the car radio just as it begins to rain. You would surely like to slide around in it and dance. "I got a woman." Yet the dark road's glare is no bright angel. No young bartender flirting with you past closing — caressing her arms with each of your tossed bottle caps.

    his humble garden . . .
    potatoes the size
    of tumors

The Gospel of Marvin

Once in a while, I can recognize it the moment it's happening, one dimension overlapping another. Snapping a picture of the Jesus painting on the wall at the local weed dispensary, I suddenly see the reflection of my face become his third eye. And so, feeling empowered, I raise my hands to the heavens. Yet no one is healed. And the dead stay dead.

>   piss jug
>   catching the roof's leak —
>   late-morning nap

Lung Cancer

Like always, the janitor sits for his break with a cup of coffee, and I sit across from him. I light a cigarette. It's Sunday morning, and the two street sweepers outside might as well be racing each other. They can't keep up. The janitor pours half and half into his cup but doesn't stir it. It floats on top, spiraling like a galaxy. I drink mine black. He takes a sip and stretches. He hasn't shaved in days. Neither have I. He reaches into the pocket of his faded blue t-shirt. Out of habit, I slide my Bic across the table. He picks it up and spins the wheel, making a few sparks but no flame. He slides it back and then pulls out an inhaler. I want to apologize, but don't because I know he understands. We stare out the window for a minute in silence and then he tells me the fox got his chickens again.

>choke cherry blossoms —
>the scent
>of blood sausage

Grandpa's Toolshed

But now, it's mostly just a shrunken-down, sun-bleached shack sinking into the sand — this glacial moraine that got left behind thousands of years ago, followed by so many ugly scrub pines. Inside, it's a mixture of musty darkness and old sawdust. A half-dozen rusty coffee cans spill every nut and bolt ever needed to construct sheer time itself. And then ultimately, I suppose, board up its memories. But the only thing I require today is his hammer. And a nail. Just one. Long enough to bang the two of us together so tightly, this woman and I, we'll have no choice but to face one another and love. Just like he and Grandma did after the war.

>   midday sun —
>   a few clouds hung
>   with the wash

[for Sam and Bernice Bergman]

The Frugal Chef

We were discussing the state of the world when I told this real caring woman I'd recently met about one of my best friends and how he'd pretty much been all alone through this Covid, global-crisis business. No job. Very few groceries in the fridge, and the ones he did have, just terrible junk. Plus, Type-2 Diabetes. Lights off most of the time. Black mold in the corners. Hardcore porn on the computer. Naturally, she expressed sincere concern over his situation and its recipes for despair. Or even suicide. But I told her that he would be just fine — because he is like a rat, a Michigan basement rat. "My dear, he can chew his way out of a black hole," I said. "Or even Hell. He's done it many times before and he'll surely do it again, only, this time, he may need to add a few of his own bones for flavor."

       sprouting potatoes —
       the afternoon alive
       with gunshots

                              [for LaVern "Moose" Clewley]

A Mysterious Certainty

There's a new book just released I wouldn't mind checking out: *The God Equation*, by Michio Kaku, a pretty well-known Japanese physicist. I heard an interview with him over the radio in which he spoke of the book and offered his thoughts on the attempted reconciliation between Einstein's relativity and quantum mechanics, which, it seems, are somewhat at odds with one another.

He spoke of strings, quarks, gravity, dark matter, the speed of light, black holes, wormholes and, of course, the big bang. Its wondrous implications. Inevitably, God does come up in a conversation such as that. It's those times I wish I had an opportunity to snag the microphone so I could quote my old trucker friend from years back: "My heart once got all whacked out of shape by some girl whose name I never even learned. It was the best summer ever."

> Sunday drive . . .
> dandelions going
> full supernova

Dirt and Weeds

No Bach
on the jukebox . . .
so I select Johnny Cash
and talk about unemployment
with a gal named Shirley.

>Andromeda
>through binoculars —
>scent of swamp mint

Sagittarius A

They say that it is a giant black hole at the center of the Milky Way.

They say that it has a mass more than a million times greater than that of our sun.

They say that not even the light of Heaven can shine through its dense eye.

Recently, they released the first blurry image of it. I think it mostly looks like a glazed donut sitting on a bright red napkin. Eternity just a humble pastry. But, of course, it took a panel of scientists to explain it all — the mathematics and chemistries involved.

The squadron of billion-dollar telescopes its council had deployed to collectively snap a Polaroid of what appears to be nothing more than what little Billy had for breakfast for his birthday.

       reading
       Thích Nhất Hạnh
       until my mind is a plum

Time

Early-morning crows — a damp, chilly wind scraping tree limbs against the trailer. I dip a cracker in my coffee until it becomes so soft, even an unborn baby could chew it. But I haven't the minutes to argue about religion or politics right now because there are many chores that must be done before the deep snow takes over. Rugs that must be smacked hard against the dark, hollow trees.

>   Year of the Tiger —
>   I stare at our dog
>   through his cataracts

Post-War Dance

My father has no idea of what is happening. He is an old man. He sits in his handicap recliner in the corner of the living room. Compares what he remembers with what's out the window. And on television. All the mess. And trust me, he knows ugliness. Vietnam and how it eventually became slivers of glass. For years it would come right up out of his skin. Possibly his exposure to Agent Orange, the V.A. doctors said. But he keeps watching the news for a more substantive answer. For the actual bones of his daily pain. He'd just like to be a kid again and go fishing with my uncles. Then light a campfire in the middle of the swamp and Crow Hop beneath the stars, like his ancient Odawa relatives did for thousands of years. With lightning in his eyes. Thunder in his chest. Stuff that doesn't require being put on a charger because it's out of life.

> golden dawn . . .
> an army of dust motes
> to catch its light

Success

Maybe my parents just keep thinking that I'm going to save my very best for last. That my "3 Year" sobriety token will soon take an even deeper hold and make me into a full-on, undisputed, real-life miracle. "He's only momentarily sitting in a broken chair wearing a urine-stained bib. He'll spring up soon enough. Give him time to become someone like Crazy Horse and unleash his thunderbirds on the glazed eyes of so many greedy, soulless men."

My grandmother, Red Bird Woman, truly believed that I could one day become another Elvis Presley and even further liberate the spirit of the Lord (the Great Spirit) from the many cold books of theology. But she died of cancer back in 1989. Four days and nights, I kept a sacred fire for the memories, the hot sparks covering my chest and shoulders like burning rhinestones.

> winter stars —
> I inhale the darkness
> and a pack of smokes

[*for Rose Wabsey Chambers*]

March Madness

When I tried to pray this morning, I wasn't really sure of what to say or ask for. So, for several minutes, I just sat on the edge of the bed, cloudy and numb, bowing my head — not in humility — but raw defeat. Tomorrow's my daughter's twentieth birthday. What could she possibly want amid this modern-day plague and societal breakdown that might be of any actual value to her? A tarot deck to help her navigate her own depths — as well as those of the stars? A flowery scarf to keep them wrapped nicely together? Cash for a couple of full tanks of gas? A shiny phone that can map out all the pockets of the diminishment. Yellow roses? A pound of weed, along with a year's worth of ramen noodles?

At this point, I'm leaning toward the smoke and groceries. She loves the Beatles, and so I'd also considered adding to her iTunes. But — too many of those songs too easily remind of the depths of the horror we're now in because they speak so profoundly about the delicate beauty outside this horror. And that wouldn't be much of a gift.

> cold night —
> with an old pocketknife
> I stir my instant coffee

Mud and Beer

Sometimes, I think the stains on my old pillow tell the stories more sharply than any of my poems. The one that looks like a crazed, homeless god was the result of a good time that somehow went haywire.

> crushed crabapples—
> his pockets heavy
> with the wind

Notes On Almost Every Despair

"In a world gushing blood day and night, you never stop mopping up pain."
— Aberjhani, *The River of Winged Dreams*

Sunday. I arrive at work and punch in. Check my daily schedule. Take a picture of it. Walk across the lobby while smiling at a man that looks confused and scared. Step into the janitor's closet and begin coming up with a plan for cleaning the whole damn building from front to back — all of it. For making it shine like beauty itself. Like sheer time shimmering on a quiet lake. But then I quickly decide that it's simply too much to accomplish.

>rising sun —
>the earth just sits there
>in a wheelbarrow

So many crows. I don't think I've ever seen this many at once before. They're traveling north, which confuses me because it's only going to become colder and deadlier the further they get. Probably the queen of all of them is hunkered down up there somewhere. Maybe in the parking lot of The Grand Hotel on Mackinaw Island. Behind a dumpster. Waiting for her soldiers to come and feed her a half-eaten tuna melt. To line up and then bow before kissing her twisted claws.

> harvest moon —
> the broom's bristles
> stiff and short

My father smacks the television remote against his temple and begins to chuckle. "It's the only way I can get this worthless junk to work," he says. He is watching the evening news. He is watching everything.

Time is yet his reward. More war. More rape. More disease. More starvation. More grinding teeth. More dirt-caked bones. And then a Viagra commercial.

> The void wants you to come out and play.
> The void wants you to come out and play.
> It knows you better than anyone.
> Black clouds are shapeshifting into black clouds.
> They look like starlings in the cold wind.
> They look like mountains fading.

At the end of the day, all I could do about anything was light one of my dollar-store Jesus candles and pray. Deeply. To God, yes, but also to dust and shadows. Memories themselves. Then I lit a cigarette like I'd just finished making love and stared at the cobwebs on the ceiling. The one that I've named "Angel" has sure been there for me.

> broken jukebox . . .
> she asks if I remember
> the words to our song

Acknowledgements

Roadside Raven Review: "Old Crow Charlie", "Dear John", "Victory Song", "The Makings of Kid Rock", "Civil War", "Chicago", "Shush", "Chinese Zen Poem", "Surviving Antarctica", "Buddha Hood", "Frugal to the End", "Nearing Profound Heights", "War Song", "Message to My Sister", "Weighing the Day's Gospels", "Blind, Empty, Odorless", "My Personal Church Pew", "The Toothless Buddha", "Antique Feminism", "Gray and Muted Landscape", "Sad Story", "Dark Winter", "1970 Something", "Recipes from the South", "Journal Entry of a Former Town Drunk", "Mother", "Oh Just a Book", "The Makings of a Medicine Man", "Death Poem", "Hubble Spots Jesus", "Chinese Zen Poem II", "Cold", "Romance in the Trenches", "Hallelujah 2019", "Grandpa's Toolshed", "Post-War Dance".

MacQueen's Quinterly: "Life Out of Balance", "A Copper Country Romance", "Lost and Found", "Health Expo", "Prayer", "The Upper Peninsula of Michigan".

Contemporary Haibun Online: "Sober", "An Ex-Lover's Birthday", "Spring Sunshine", "Notes to My Daughter", "He Who Knows Nothing Lasts", "A Mysterious Certainty", "March Madness".

Drifting Sands: "Untitled", "Notes On Almost Every Despair".

Red River Review: "Irene".

Dunes Review: "Lung Cancer" (Winner of the William J. Shaw Memorial Prize).

Failed Haiku: "Mud and Beer".

ANDREW RIUTTA was born and raised in the Upper Peninsula of Michigan. He is a father, chef, and Zamboni operator. His essay "The Myths of Manhood," from the collection *This I Believe: On Fatherhood* (Jossey-Bass), was featured on Public Radio International's Bob Edwards Show in 2012.